JN204047

A PROMISE TO LIVE FOR

The story of how two small children had to trek
all alone across Manchuria in 1946

Izumi Mochizuki Greubel

Illustrated by Ikue"Iku"Mochizuki
Translated by Douglas Mochizuki Greubel

PENCOM

In Shizuoka (1939)
Iku's Grandma and Grandpa (In circle sitting down)
Mommy with Misa (front row sitting down, the first lady on the right)
Iku (next to Mommy with a hat)
Daddy (standing behind Iku)
Uncle So (the second person in the back row in dark school uniform)
Aunt Yuki (the lady standing in the back row next to Daddy)

To my mother
and
grandmother,
this book is dedicated to you.
Together we pray for world peace…

"War makes murderers out of otherwise decent people.
All wars, and all decent people."

--Benjamin Ferencz

(the last surviving prosecutor at the Nuremberg trials)

I am Iku and I'm going to tell you a story. It is the true story of how my little brother and I crossed a very dangerous expanse of Manchuria all alone… a long time ago, in 1946. Our story is also a story of war. Not of who's on the right side and who's on the wrong side, or who was crueler than the other, but how the consequences of war can impact people everywhere-- people like you and me. Most importantly, this is a story of how love, courage and determination can see us all through hard times.

CONTENTS

1946 September 3 - September 30: Tonghua ~ Huludao Port

1946 September 30 - October 9: On the Ship

1946 October 9: Sasebo Port

1946 October 13: Shizuoka

2016 New Year Holidays: Shizuoka

The Journey of Iku and Kiyoshi

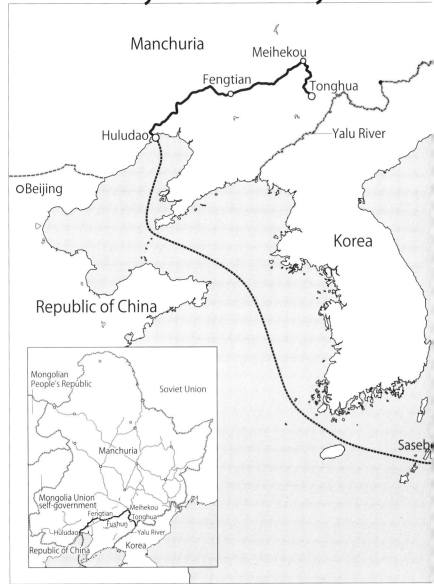

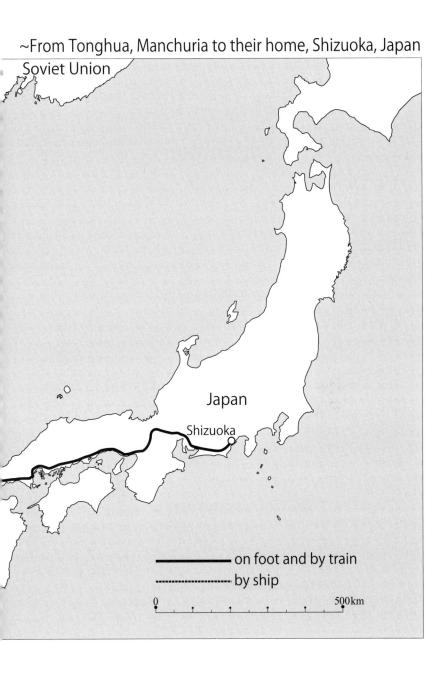

~From Tonghua, Manchuria to their home, Shizuoka, Japan

Soviet Union

Japan

Shizuoka

———— on foot and by train
------------------ by ship

0   500km

2016 New Year Holidays:

Shizuoka

Prologue

"I bet you're all hungry! Come on in! I've made some onigiri.[1]"

On the last day of winter break, five grandchildren were playing ball games in the backyard while Grandma called out to them. She is petite and charming, turning eighty this year. Her soft, pink sweater suits her very well.

"Yay! She said she has onigiri!"

"Gotta wash our hands!"

"I already washed them."

---

1   onigiri: It's a Japanese rice ball with triangle or round shapes and usually wrapped with a sheet of seaweed. It's also called omusubi.

"But not with soap!"

As the children gathered around the table, they could not contain their excitement for Grandma's onigiri. The children gobbled down their food as Grandma sat down next to Kai, the youngest grandchild.

"Mmm… Grandma, it's so yummy!"

"Grandma's onigiri are kind of different from Mom's. They're so white, round, and fluffy."

"Yeah, white, round, and fluffy," everyone agreed.

"White, round, and fluffy…"

Grandma said softly as she quietly looked off into the distance.

"Grandma, is everything ok?" said Kai worriedly.

"White, round, and fluffy… when I heard that phrase, it reminded me of a time when I was called Iku," said Grandma.

"Iku? What a cute name!"

"I was just around Kai's age when I lived in an area called Manchuria[2] in China," explained Grandma.

"Manchuria?"

"Yes, Manchuria. At the time, Japan was at war and was trying to expand their territory. An area that was a little north of Beijing and spread to the border with Russia was called Manchuria. During the war, many Japanese families moved there."

"Oh, I didn't know that."

---

2   Manchuria (also known as Manchukou): Japan invaded this part of China located in northeast China and started governing it in 1932. At the general assembly of the League of Nations in 1933, Manchuria was not recognized as a part of Japan and the Japanese military were told to leave the region. The Japanese government, however, decided to withdraw from the League of Nations and to continue governing Manchuria. Japan rapidly built and developed railroads, mines, ports, hospitals, schools, and the infrastructure of Manchuria. Many Japanese families moved to Manchuria, including teachers, workers, businessmen, shopkeepers, and military officers. Most big cities in Manchuria had large Japanese business districts and residential neighborhoods. There were also many Japanese farmers and their families who moved to Manchuria to farm the region's large fertile land.

"My father, your great grandfather, was a civil engineer who designed bridges, dams, and buildings. He was asked to construct bridges over a river that divides current day North Korea and China called the Yalu River. That meant that my whole family, including my father, mother, brothers and sisters, we all lived in Manchuria, but…"

Grandma's eyes filled with sorrow as she looked at the onigiri, and she slowly started to tell the story of when she was called Iku.

Iku's mother and father's wedding photo (1935)

1942 End of the Year:

Shizuoka ~ Tonghua

Pipe Tobacco and Dried Bananas

"Only a few more days until the New Year!"

I was skipping and singing in the garden under the warm sun while Grandpa puffed at his pipe tobacco. In the months since I last saw Mommy and Daddy, I had become a kindergartener, and every year since preschool, I couldn't wait for the New Year. That holiday was especially exciting for me because that was when my parents would return from Manchuria.

Daddy was a civil engineer. When I was three years old, he had been asked to design bridges over the Yalu River in Manchuria. Mommy and Daddy decided to only take my little sister, Misa, with them.

"Iku, you're a big girl now. You will be staying with Grandma and Grandpa here in Shizuoka. Can you promise me you'll be on your best behavior?" asked Daddy as I nodded.

Iku (2-yr. old), Misa (4-mo. old)

Even though I was left by myself, I was determined to keep my promise to Daddy and to behave myself as best as I could everyday while staying at Grandma and Grandpa's.

I walked home holding hands with my cousin Masaki every day from kindergarten. Every afternoon, Grandma and Grandpa would hear me come home while I excitedly opened the door and asked, "Did Mommy and Daddy come home yet?"

Last year when they came home for the New Year, I met my baby brother Kiyoshi for the first time. I couldn't wait to play with Misa and Kiyoshi, and to teach them all of my favorite songs that I had learned at school.

I continued to pester Grandpa, asking when Mommy and Daddy were coming home. His answer was always filled with uncertainty. To take my mind off sadness, Grandpa would give me a snack and take me for a walk. Of course, Masaki would always go along. Me on the right and Masaki on the left, hanging onto Grandpa's big, rough hands, we would walk among the rice paddies. The faint, familiar smell of Grandpa's tobacco would follow us. I always loved those walks, so filled with adventure that they seemed like treasure hunts--picking horsetail flowers, catching minnows and tadpoles, and watching dragon flies whiz by.

As the sun began to set, Masaki's mother would arrive to pick him up.

"Iku, let's play again tomorrow!"

"Sure! See you!"

I would quietly watch Masaki hold his mother's hand as they walked home under the fading orange sky. I felt my heart sink and began to feel more and more sorrow as the sun disappeared in the distance. I would rush to Grandma and held on tightly to her.

"Grandma? Why can't Mommy be at home with me? When are they coming home? I want to see them… I want to hold hands with Mommy…"

At times like these, Grandma would soothe the ache in my heart with a soft lullaby.

I was always excited when Uncle So came home from high school, because he taught me many songs, how to count, and how to read characters while holding me on his lap. Thanks to Uncle So, I could even read a clock.

Aunt Yuki, who attended a sewing school, had made beautiful outfits for me.

"I chose your favorite color pink this time. Quick! Try it on!"

"Wow, it even has two pockets! I can put both of my hands in here!"

"It fits you perfectly! Next time I'll make you a coat to go with it, ok?"

I proudly walked off to kindergarten every day wearing my favorite dress hand made by Aunt Yuki.

Iku (on the left with a bonnet, 3 ½-yr. old)
Uncle So (on the far right)
Aunt Yuki (next to Uncle So)

Whenever my class put on a play, Grandma always showed up and was excited to watch us sing and dance. After it finished, Masaki and I both held hands with Grandma as we walked home.

"Both of you did such an amazing job with the dances. I especially loved the Seagull Dance. You looked so cute. Here's a little treat."

Grandma pulled out two small gifts wrapped in handkerchiefs from her bag and handed them to us.

"Grandma, thank you so much!"

I grasped the handkerchief with both hands and gently brought it closer to my nose as I closed my eyes. The slightly tart yet sweet aroma filled my nose and spread through my chest.

Mmm... that's what I thought... dried bananas...

They weren't the ordinary dried persimmons or dried sweet potatoes, but rare dried bananas. I didn't know where Grandma got them from but knew Grandma had saved these luxurious snacks for special occasions. I ate them bit by bit, savoring it as long as I could.

Welcome Home

As the New Year approached, I continued to rush home every day from kindergarten to hurriedly open the door and to ask, "Are Mommy and Daddy home yet?"

"Hmm, not yet, I'm afraid," replied Grandpa as he sat at his regular spot puffing on his pipe. Grandpa's same reply was met with my usual look of disappointment as I put down my backpack. However, I saw Masaki start playing next to Grandpa and decided to play, too.

"One, two, three!"

We were playing beanbag toss. The sound of the little, dried red beans filled the room. These colorful beanbags reminded me of Mommy because she had made them before leaving for Manchuria. I felt as if I was talking with her as I heard the gentle sound of the red beans inside the beanbags.

Grandma then asked me to help her cook dinner. I was put in charge of keeping the stove fire[3] strong and hot.

"Iku, blow a little harder, please!" asked Grandma while I was blowing into the flame with my small bamboo pipe. However, sooner or later, the smoke began hurting my eyes so I ran out to get some fresh air. As I was rubbing my eyes, I noticed some people's silhouettes approaching in the distance.

"Grandma! Someone's coming!"

---

3   stove fire: In early 1940 in Japan, it was still very common to prepare meals on the hearth using fire wood. A hollow piece of wood, such as bamboo, was used to get the fire going by blowing air into it.

One of the people suddenly started waving his hand at me.

Daddy? Yes? No?... YES!!

"It's Daddy! They came home!"

Between Mommy and Daddy was Misa, waving her hand just like Daddy. I saw Daddy holding on to Kiyoshi. I ran at a full sprint to the front of the house to welcome them.

"Daddy! Mommy!"

I couldn't contain my excitement and called out as I hopped up and down.

"Good, good…" said Grandpa as he came out the front door with Grandma following closely behind.

"Father, Mother, we have returned. Both of you look to be in great health and we are all so thankful for your hospitality," said Daddy to his parents-in-law.

Then, Daddy turned his attention to me and gently patted my head saying, "Iku, we came home. Thank you for being so strong while we were gone."

Misa clung on to Daddy's leg and shyly hid behind him. Misa and I just stared at each other and then exchanged shy smiles with each other.

"Iku, thank you for staying behind and being such a good girl. You've grown taller!" said Mommy. I noticed that Mommy had a nenneko[4] on her back. Inside that nenneko was my seven-month old baby brother Hiro. I had become the proud big sister of four siblings.

---

4   nenneko: It's a short cape-like coat to cover a baby on mother's back and is mainly used in winter.

That evening was lively and filled with joy. Around the dinner table, Daddy had explained recent news in Manchuria as well as his work. There was so much news to catch up on. Kiyoshi had missed his homeland's rice so much that he even asked for a second helping. By the end of the night, there was no left-over food and everyone's belly was full as much as their hearts were with happiness.

After the bath, I got ready for bed and quietly said good-night to Grandma and Grandpa. Then I headed to the bedroom where Mommy was putting Baby Hiro to sleep. I hopped into the futon[5] right next to Mommy and snuggled closely under the warm blanket.

"Mommy..."

I was comforted by Mommy's familiar scent that filled my chest as I searched for Mommy's soft,

---

5   futon: This is the traditional Japanese bedding before western beds were introduced to Japan. Futon is usually prepared on the tatami mat on the floor. A futon set is folded and stored in a closet during the day to allow the room to be used for other purposes. It was not uncommon for a Japanese family to lay on an individual futon for each family member in the same room and sleep together, especially while the children were small.

warm hand. In the dark room, I squeezed Mommy's hand. Mommy gently squeezed back.

That night, my heart was so content.

Iku with Mommy, Kiyoshi and Hiro

New Year Celebration

New Year's Day[6] was filled with exciting activities and amazing food. We ate ozoni and osechi[7] -- lots of them. We flew our kites high up in the air, played with hanetsuki[8], and everyone had a great time. We took an annual family photograph for this special occasion.

While she was busy helping out in the kitchen or sewing clothes, Mommy seemed to love watching her children's energetic play.

Daddy was a fan of classical music and could often be seen listening to his favorite records in one of the private rooms. When I needed a break from playing with my siblings and cousins, I loved to silently approach Daddy and to sit on his lap, so I, too, could

---

6   New Year's Day in Japan: It's the biggest and most important event celebrated in Japan on January 1 and lasting for several days. There are many traditional customs, food, and games for this special occasion.

7   ozoni, osechi: These are the special dishes prepared for the New Year celebration in Japan.

8   hanetsuki: It is one of the traditional Japanese games played during the New Year celebration along with flying kites and card games. Hanetsuki is similar to badminton.

enjoy the relaxing melodies. Daddy's favorite was "La Traviata" and it also became my favorite. It was such a special moment for Daddy and me.

One evening after the main three days of the New Year celebration were over, Daddy asked the family to gather and sit down.

"Iku, you're almost a first grader now. When we return to Manchuria this time, I want you to join us. In April[9], you can attend the Japanese School of Manchuria as a first grader!" said Daddy.

"I get to go with you this time? I don't have to stay behind anymore? Can Grandma and Grandpa come with us?" I asked.

"Unfortunately, no… Grandma and Grandpa already have their home here, so they won't be coming with us."

I glanced over at Mommy. She nodded to me with her familiar, sweet smile.

"Grandma and I will be waiting for you here

9   April: Japanese school year goes from April to March.

until you return. You'll be a first grader in Manchuria, Iku. How exciting!" said Grandpa.

You know what? I get to hold Mommy's hand every night when I sleep!

I couldn't be happier with that thought. I was so excited to be back with the whole family again and to imagine the new adventure which was about to start at a place called Manchuria.

Iku (5-yr. old), Misa (3 ½-yr. old)

Let's Go!

The day had come to leave for Manchuria. After breakfast, Misa and I were playing hopscotch in the front yard until Mommy called out for us.

"Iku! Misa! Come on in and change your clothes! Today you will both be wearing especially pretty dresses."

"Ok, we're coming!" We energetically replied. As we both stepped inside, we saw a set of matching dresses that Aunt Yuki had made and had neatly folded.

"Yay! We are going out! We are going out!!"

Misa started singing in excitement as she put the pretty dress on, and twirled in circles. Misa and I had a photo taken in our red dresses in the front yard.

Iku (on the right, 6 ½-yr. old), Misa (4-yr. old)

"Iku, we need you to help us carry one of the backpacks. Can you handle it?"

"Yep, of course!"

Even though I was almost a first grader, the backpack proved to be a little big and heavy for my small frame.

"Uh oh!"

I started to lean too far back, but with help of Mommy I was able to regain my footing. On Mommy's back was Baby Hiro, and holding her hand tightly was two-year old Kiyoshi.

Daddy took a moment to kneel at the family altar[10]. He gave thanks to our ancestors and prayed for safe travels. After neatly tying his shoes, he picked up a very heavy looking bag and said his farewells to Grandma and Grandpa.

---

10 family altar: It's called Butsudan. In Japanese Buddhist culture, each house has a small wood altar and family members often burn incense and say quiet prayers to their ancestors and loved ones.

"Thank you very much for your continuous hospitality. We will head out now. Please take good care of yourselves."

Mommy and Daddy bowed deeply toward them.

"Grandma, Grandpa, see you later! I promise to write lots of letters. Please make sure to come visit us sometime!" I said.

"Iku, take care of yourself and good luck at your new school! Here, take these snacks with you," said Grandma. I received the snack that Grandma had wrapped in a handkerchief. I brought it up to my nose and instantly recognized the sweet scent.

"Dried bananas! Grandma, thank you!"

Mommy and Daddy bowed their heads deeply once again as we departed.

As we walked down the road, I turned to look one last time at Grandma and Grandpa. Grandma was dabbing her eyes with the sleeves of her kimono.

"Grandma, take care!" I screamed.

"Grandma, take care!" Misa screamed.

"You copycat!"

We giggled at each other as we followed closely behind Mommy and Daddy.

The whole family boarded a train at the main railway station in Shizuoka[11] and the journey was filled with tunnels and stops. Once we finally got off the train, we then boarded a large ship.

We, especially children, were excited at the beginning, but started getting bored after spending four, five days on the ship.

"Are we there yet?"

Daddy decided to take me to the ship's deck to pass the time. I kept gazing at the vast sea before us.

Suddenly someone yelled.

11   Shizuoka-city: It's located in the central part of Honshu and is 100 miles southwest of Tokyo. It is near Mt. Fuji.

"Look! I can see land!"

I turned my head to take a look and sure enough I saw land in the distance.

"Daddy, is that Manchuria?" I asked.

"Yes, that is Manchuria. Our home awaits us there," replied Daddy.

The New Home

For the first time in my life, I set foot in this new land called Manchuria. Even the faint breeze smelled differently from Japan.

My family boarded another train to our home, a city called Tonghua[12]. My siblings and I continued to eat some snacks and dozed on and off from the soft vibrations of the train until we finally reached Tonghua Station. As we stepped off the station's platform, there were plenty of horse-drawn carriages waiting for customers. My family hopped into the closest carriage and then the horse trotted off.

---

12   Tonghua: It's located in the south of Jilin Province in China bordering North Korea.

It's so cold!

Even though we were wearing winter coats, January winters in Manchuria were extremely cold. The carriage had a cover but the cold wind was still hitting our faces. Misa and I turned away from the wind and sat as close to each other as we could to stay warm.

After about fifteen minutes, the carriage came to a stop on Gaolong Street. I saw our house for the first time.

"Hello… anybody home?"

I nervously said in a small voice and stepped in to a quiet house. From behind, Misa and Kiyoshi ran in, flung their shoes off[13], and went in saying, "We're home!"

I looked around and noticed that it wasn't large, but rather more like a regular Japanese-style house.

---

13   shoes off: It's one of the Japanese customs to take their shoes off as they enter homes. At the entranceway, they take their shoes off and leave them there, then enter the main part of the house which is about a foot or two higher.

"Iku, come over here!"

Misa called for me. Misa wanted to show me around the house and we did a circle. Next was outside. We stepped out the backdoor and there was a large valley with a small local village on the other side.

I looked up at the blue sky, closed my eyes, and took in a big, deep breath of the cold Manchurian air. My chest was filled with excitement as my new life in Manchuria was about to start.

Manchuria

A few days after arriving in Tonghua, I accompanied Daddy to the city center. It was an extremely well developed Japanese town, with restaurants, stores and Japanese signs everywhere. There were even post offices, hospitals and banks. I noticed a lady wearing kappogi[14] shopping for vegetables as well as several Japanese soldiers riding

---

14   kappogi: It's a kind of apron with long sleeves, mainly worn to protect kimono from getting dirty and stained.

around on horseback. Japanese language was heard everywhere. It was just like being in Japan.

Several months passed and April had come around. I was experiencing my first spring in Manchuria, and it was time for me to enroll in the Japanese elementary school with other children in my neighborhood. I didn't have to walk to school. Daddy arranged for a local Chinese man to drop me off at school in the morning and pick me up from school in the afternoon on a carriage. I passed by beautiful cherry blossoms that were at full bloom on the way to school and had so much fun every day.

At school, I learned how to read and write in Japanese, and I picked up Chinese outside of school. My carriage driver taught me how to count in Chinese.

"Yi, Er, San, Si, Wu, Liu, Qi, Ba, Jiu, Shi!"

I excitedly repeated my counting over and over. After school, I would often go out to the fields with Misa and my school friends to pick dandelions and clovers and then we pretended to make fancy hair accessories and jewelry.

There were local Chinese men and women carrying a pole selling food. All the children, including me, loved these local snacks. The sweet potatoes were so juicy that I could almost see the syrup dripping through the basket.

That being said, Daddy prohibited us from buying anything from the locals.

One day, I couldn't resist buying a mantou[15], and when I did, I knew I had made a mistake. I was caught by Daddy.

"Didn't I tell you can never buy and eat that kind of food? We Japanese[16] don't eat such food!" yelled Daddy. After being scolded, I sat at the corner of the room very downhearted.

---

15   mantou: It's a Chinese steamed bun made out of wheat flour or corn mill. They are very dense, and usually don't have any fillings in them.

16   We Japanese: Daddy's generation often looked down on other Asian countries and their people when Japan invaded and occupied them during World War II.

"Iku, here, open your mouth," Mommy softly spoke and gave me a konpeitou, a small Japanese candy that is shaped like a star.

Another long winter had passed since arriving in Manchuria. I became a second grader and Misa a first grader. The two of us happily went to school every day, each of us with our own lunch boxes that Mommy had prepared for us. Soon the newest addition to the family was born, a baby brother. He was called Little Shige. After coming home from school every day, Misa and I were busy helping Mommy take care of our three little brothers.

Daddy's colleague and neighbor, Mr. Akai and his wife, Mrs. Akai, were always willing to give a hand to the busy mother of five.

"I steamed lots of pumpkin today and we can't eat all of it. Please take some."

"I was able to get lots of beans today at the market. Here you go."

The Akai's were always so thoughtful toward my family. In fact, they adored Misa so much that Mr. Akai asked Daddy whether they could adopt her because they did not have any children of their own.

We were all far away from home, but the Japanese community in Manchuria continued to thrive by helping each other out. Even though the country was at war, there was a sufficient food supply and everyone was living peacefully together.

1945 Summer:

Tonghua

The Day Japan Lost the War

August 15th, 1945 was a day that was no different from other days for us children. The sun was bright as usual and it was another hot summer day. Sunflowers were brightly reflecting the sunlight off their golden petals in the valley in the back of the house. Mr. and Mrs. Akai had come over in the morning and they were discussing something with Mommy and Daddy. They all looked rather tense.

At around lunch time, Daddy called for all of us children to gather.

"Sit down here," he said sternly. Sitting on top of the cupboard was a radio, and Mr. and Mrs. Akai had already sat down in front of it. My siblings and I followed suit and sat down next to them. Mommy and Daddy were sitting closely behind while we all waited for the radio broadcast to begin.

The radio suddenly came to life. As the static began to fade away, a man's voice could be heard as he began his speech. The man on the radio was using so many difficult words that I had no idea what he was talking about.

As I glanced up, all I saw were extremely stiffened expressions across the adults' faces. I started to worry that something extremely awful had occurred. The broadcast ended abruptly and was followed by silence. Daddy finally spoke up while choking on his words.

"… Japan lost…"

For years and years, the Japanese military's achievements and progressions were proudly written all over the papers. The Japanese people believed that the "Country of God: Japan" was destined to win, but for Japan to lose…

On that very day of August 15th, as a requirement of Japan's surrender, Manchuria no longer belonged to Japan. There were no more "high level" Japanese people and "low level" Chinese people--the former Japanese order crumbled. Some Chinese burst out their suppressed frustration and many ugly incidents, big and small, unfolded throughout Manchuria.

Misa and I were no longer able to attend the Japanese school. The carriage driver that had taught me Chinese never came back after August 15th.

Daddy's office had been shut down and he was forced to find work elsewhere. Even Mommy had to go and find work on some days as well.

The stores and vendors that were managed by Japanese people were also shut down, and the number of Japanese people walking on the streets decreased greatly. The Japanese soldiers that used to be everywhere suddenly disappeared.

Since all of the banks were closed, withdrawing money became impossible and everyone was struggling to find any cash. To make ends meet, people were forced to sell their clothes, pots, furniture, and so much more of their personal belongings in order to survive day by day. At home, I noticed that Mommy's beautiful kimonos were disappearing one by one.

The end of the war drastically changed the life of the Japanese people that were left in Manchuria.

Their lives were turned upside down. Even though the war was officially over, for many Japanese in Manchuria, including my family, it was only the beginning of the battle.

A Large, Large Hole

One day while I was helping Mommy bring in the laundry, we suddenly heard an airplane. Since I had moved to Manchuria, I was not accustomed to air raids as the people in Japan were. Even the neighboring children had wandered outside kind of excited about the sound of an airplane.

I wonder which country that airplane is from…

The children continued to stare at the shiny plane that flew by. I stepped inside with Mommy to fold my brother's cloth diapers. Suddenly, the noise of the airplane started to get louder again.

"It's coming here again!"

Misa and Kiyoshi stuck their heads out the window to search for the plane.

It was at that moment.

BOOM!

The sound of an enormous explosion that no one had ever heard before shook the whole house like an earthquake.

"Mommy!"

I instantly covered my ears and ran to Mommy's lap. Misa and Kiyoshi fled from the window and curled up on the floor. No one dared to move out of fear. It seemed like so much time had passed before I hesitantly raised my head to check our surroundings.

Voices of many worried people could be heard outside.

What just happened?

I had to find out and made my way to the front door. I looked over to where everyone was crowding around. Diagonally across from our house in the middle of the road was a large, large hole in the ground. A bomb had been dropped.

"Mommy, Mommy! There's a huge hole over by where Mr. Kimura's house is!" I screamed. Luckily no one was injured nor were any houses damaged, but this ominous event was not taken lightly.

The Empty House

Due to Japan having lost the war, the Japanese people left behind in Manchuria were less safe as each day passed.

I want to go back to Japan…

Despite waiting for such a long time, the Japanese families in Manchuria still had not received any word when they would be able to return to Japan. That being said, no one lost hope. All families had prepared backpacks and trunks filled with essentials, hidden away in attics and under the floor so they could leave immediately if necessary.

Cash was often cleverly hidden away in pillows or sewn into kimono collars to prevent theft.

One day when both Mommy and Daddy had left for a day job, my siblings and I were quietly staying home.

Suddenly,

BAM!

The front door flung open.

Who's there?

I was startled by the sudden sound and quickly turned my head as Chinese soldiers barged into our home with their boots on. All of the soldiers had blank looks which made them look even scarier.

I was too terrified to scream. All of us siblings ran into the corner of the room where we huddled and shook in fear. The soldiers started rummaging through our belongings, emptying our drawers and closets, and even flipping over the tatami[17]. They gathered up everything they liked, including our study desk and cupboard, and hauled it all away.

The soldiers also managed to find our trunks that were hidden underneath the floor and took them away with them. However, luckily, they did not find

17   tatami: Tatami mats are used as a flooring material in traditional Japanese rooms. They are made from rice straw and soft rush straw. One tatami mat measures about 2 yards by 1 yard with about 2 inches of thickness.

another trunk and two large backpacks hidden away in the attic. Although the amount of time that the soldiers spent inside the house might have been quite short, for me, it felt as if they were there for two, maybe three fear-filled hours.

After the soldiers finally left, the house was empty and no one was able to speak and break the silence. Baby Shige, who was a year and a half old, finally began to whimper and it was only then that we returned to our senses. We looked at each other and realized that we were all covered in sweat.

Mommy arrived home from work soon after.

"I'm home."

As soon as she opened the door, she instantly realized what had occurred. Most of the household belongings were gone, the tatami mats were upside down, and what was left behind was a cluttered mess.

"Iku, Misa, Kiyoshi, Hiro, Shige!" Mommy frantically called and searched for us.

"Mommy!!"

At the very end of the hallway, she found us all huddled into one corner. At that very moment, Mommy lost all her strength and sank to the floor.

A Little Mommy

During these chaotic times in Manchuria, Mommy gave birth to her sixth child. Born far before the due date, she was a tiny baby girl. My new baby sister was so weak that she did not even have the strength to drink Mommy's milk. Later that night, she silently let out her last tiny breath.

The next morning, Daddy quietly made a fire in the back yard and cremated[18] the baby. He then picked up her tiny bones and placed them inside a little pot. With Baby Shige on my back, I watched Daddy's sorrowful back from behind.

Mommy's health worsened after giving birth. It was becoming more and more difficult for her to get out of bed every day. This meant that I, then nine years old, had to take over for Mommy, including cooking, laundry, and taking care of my siblings all at once. Although I was quite small for my age, I was still the oldest sister. I became a little mommy.

After washing breakfast dishes, it was time to bring a washtub to Mommy's bedside, and then to go back and forth with a bucket to fill enough water in the washtub.

---

18   cremated: Traditionally in Japan, bodies are cremated instead of buried in a casket.

"One, two, one, two…"

Being careful not to spill any water, I steadily carried a bucket. While chatting next to Mommy who was sitting up on her futon bed, Mommy and I did laundry together.

Once washing the clothes was complete, it was time to take it all outside to rinse. Misa would often help out as well.

After everything was well rinsed, it was time to get up on my tippy-toes to hang all the shirts and diapers on the clothes line. With Baby Shige on my back, it was a demanding task for me.

As evening fell, it was time again to carry whimpering Baby Shige on my back and go to the backyard to prepare dinner.

Using an oil drum as a substitute for a cooking stove, I placed the firewood underneath our makeshift pot. With limited food supplies, we mostly ate congee made with corn and koryan[19]. Koryan was infamous for being extremely hard and tough to eat, no matter how long it was cooked.

I wish I could eat a whole big bowl of white rice…

We were hungry every day.

---

19   koryan: Its English name is sorghum, also called millet and milo. Its grain is used for food for humans and animals.

The Refugees

Fortunately, no one chased my family away from our home. However, many Japanese who were living in the northern parts of Manchuria faced the Soviet army[20]. They had to give up their homes and farmland as they sought shelter further south.

Even in Tonghua, the former schools, hotels, and various other buildings were now used as shelter for the Japanese refugees. I started hearing many stories from Daddy about these refugees who ran for their lives after losing everything.

I heard that shortly before these Japanese people were forced to leave their homes, the group leaders handed out sickles and cyanide[21] tablets to everyone in

---

20   Soviet army: On August 9, 1945, a week before the WWII ended, the Soviet Union broke the Soviet-Japanese Neutrality Pact and declared war against Japan. The Soviet Army invaded Manchuria from the north. Many Japanese families who were living in the northern part of Manchuria ran for their lives. The most famous incident "Gegenmiao Massacre" happened on August 14. The Soviet Army shot, raped, and ran over Japanese people with tanks. Over 1000 people, mostly women and children, were killed during this 2-hour ordeal.

21   cyanide: It's a chemical compound and very toxic. Japanese people were taught back then that taking their own lives was far better than being captured or killed by their enemies.

order to prepare themselves for the worst-case scenario, should they not be able to run away from enemy forces. In fact, there were many people who decided to take their own lives in despair, refusing to be taken as prisoners or to be killed by enemies. Women were told to shave their heads and paint their faces with charcoal or mud to resemble men while seeking refuge. While in hiding, mothers would be forced to cover and muffle their crying babies' mouths in fear of being found, only to find that their babies had lost their lives. Other mothers found themselves being forced to give away or sell their children to local Chinese people. So many children were orphaned and even got lost during the treacherous journey.

I saw the refugees arriving in Tonghua with virtually no belongings, with only the clothes on their back if they were fortunate. For some, they had to resort to hemp fabric, intended for rice and wheat storage, to wear some sort of makeshift clothing. Their lives were even tougher than my family's as they were literally running for their lives.

Surviving through the harsh winter proved to be incredibly brutal. Without being able to cultivate any crops, there were days when people were not able to find any food. Many children, elderly, and the weak, were constantly falling due to illness and malnutrition. Diseases like typhus spread through the communities and people were dying every day.

Even though people wanted to bury their lost loved ones, all the surrounding land was already filled with mounds and mounds of graves. Even if they did find some space, the dirt was always frozen during the winter with no way of digging a hole for a proper burial. Desperate attempts to cover bodies with leaves and dirt were not an uncommon sight. Sadly, these bodies were only to be dug up by hungry stray dogs and wolves soon after.

Behind my house, the once beautiful valley was now filled with fresh graves that continued to increase every day. Once the sun set, blueish white fireballs[22] were seen flying off in the distance.

---

22   blueish white fireballs: These fireballs must have been created by chemical reactions from the cremated bodies. Iku remembers these small fireballs flying in the valley.

1946 Winter:

Tonghua

The Incident on Chinese New Year

Four months have passed since the end of the war, and the New Year arrived quietly. It was now 1946, but there were no hints of any celebrations taking place. Nor were there any special foods or clothes for the New Year festivities. My family ate our usual koryan congee on New Year's Day, but we were lucky enough to have a few sweet potatoes mixed in as a treat for the special day.

About one month later, February 3rd was the Chinese New Year. On this special day, a dramatic incident occurred in Tonghua, later known as the

Tonghua Incident. It was a day that affected many Japanese families and my family was no exception.

On the morning of February 3rd, the streets suddenly filled with noise. Then our front door was violently opened and several Chinese soldiers in heavy boots barged in. I ran to Mommy. The soldiers began yelling at Daddy. They grabbed his arms and started dragging him out the door.

"Please stop!" Mommy screamed. A soldier glared back while he kicked over a wood crate that was being used as a table. Daddy tried to resist and to tug his arms free but the Chinese soldiers suddenly stripped him down to his underwear.

As soon as Daddy tried to fight back, they beat his shoulders with their gun butts. Within a second, two big bruises appeared on Daddy's back. All of us children clung to Mommy who, shivering in fear in the corner of the room, held on tightly to Baby Shige. Daddy's hands were bound behind his back with steel wire and he was dragged outside into -20°C (-4°F) weather.

The front door had been left wide open and freezing air quickly filled the house. Yelling and screaming could still be heard outside. With a face filled with tears and shock, I looked up at Mommy. Clutching on tightly to her children, Mommy's expression was filled with strength and determination.

I felt the cold air on my face and came to my senses.

"I'm going to close the door."

I reached for the door and looked off into the

distance, but there was no sign of Daddy. After quietly closing the door, Misa and I hid next to the window and kept watch on the outside.

Down the street on a snowy hill, we saw many men that were about Daddy's and Grandpa's age, all forced to walk handcuffed in a single file. We also saw a worried wife screaming and approaching the men being taken away.

Then suddenly,

BANG!

Without any hesitation, a gunshot was fired and the woman collapsed into the snow.

Oh my gosh!

We leaped back from the window in fear. That was not the only gunshot we heard. Gunshots were sounding everywhere. We covered our ears and ran to the comfort of Mommy.

For the next week, none of us could leave the house and quietly passed the time inside. Gunshots could still be heard. I began to worry whether Mr. Akai, who had adored Misa so much, had been taken away, or how Mrs. Akai was holding up. However, no matter how worried I was, I was afraid to take a single step outside and had no idea how my neighbors were doing.

It's Daddy!

One day during these chaotic times, Daddy suddenly came home.

"Daddy!!"

There he was, standing at the door step in tattered clothes with a blue, sunken face. There was some swelling on his face as well as some bruises. As he limped on one leg, Daddy slowly made his way into the house. When Mommy rushed to his side to help him change into more comfortable, warm clothes, she suddenly gasped.

Daddy's back was covered in dark reddish

purple bruises and swelling. His right shoulder was especially bruised to the point where he could not raise his right arm at all. He grimaced in pain as he changed into fresh clothes and slowly sat down. He sipped some warm water. After several moments of silence, Daddy began to speak little by little in his weak voice.

"On that day when we were taken, we were walking along the Hujiang River[23] where it was frozen with a thick layer of ice. There were large holes in the ice and Japanese men were forced to stand there one by one, only to be shot from behind. They all fell into the hole and sank into the cold, deep water. It was like a factory line to execute all the Japanese. On top of that, many dead bodies were left lying on the side of the streets where some of the Chinese would come and steal the clothes off of them. Naked bodies were everywhere…

… I was beginning to prepare myself for the river, but I was taken to a bomb shelter instead. It was so packed with people we couldn't even move. There was no space for a bathroom, so we had to go where

---

23   The Hujiang River: A big river running through the city of Tonghua.

we were standing. The smell was just so horrible and no one could breathe. They didn't give us any food, nor even a drop of water….

… Hours had passed, then the gate swung open and they started shooting at random. Men were falling over right before my eyes. I was able to somehow climb up and hang from the ceiling, just barely able to hide in the soldiers' blind spot. That evening, the living and the dead were locked up inside the shelter."

Daddy paused and took another sip of warm water. I noticed Daddy grimace as he switched seating positions to be able to continue.

"The next morning, the gate opened again and I thought that they would kill me for sure this time, but instead, they ordered those of us that survived to step outside. We did as we were told. By this point, I no longer felt anything. I was no longer scared. We were taken to the detention facility. Even on the short walk to the detention facility, there were dead bodies everywhere on the frozen ground. I reached the point where I didn't think twice when I saw another dead body...

... One by one we were called into the interrogation room. To find out if we sided with the Japanese rebel army,[24] we were tortured and beaten all over our backs with whips and wooden swords. No matter how much they beat me, there was nothing for me to confess. Eventually they put me back in the detention room. The sounds of whips and screams seemed to never end...

---

24   The Japanese rebel army: Later this event was named the Tonghua Incident. Over 3000 Japanese men who were living in and around Tonghua-city were all taken away as prisoners. Many were shot. Many were tortured. After a week of being tortured and not being fed in the freezing temperature, it is said that over 2000 men died.

… After a while, several other men and I were thrown out of the building. I thought the soldiers would come after us and shoot as soon as we started walking. However, they stepped back inside. On my way home I looked at the Hujiang River where frozen bodies were thrown off into the frozen river from the bridge. More naked bodies were found on the side of the road."

Daddy let out a deep sigh.

"Iku, is there any koryan left? Some congee would be great."

Several days after Daddy came home, someone slowly opened the front door.

"Hello."

I turned around and there I saw Mr. and Mrs. Akai standing at the entrance. Mr. Akai looked just as exhausted as Daddy did, but he had been safely released as well and had just arrived back home. Misa ran down the front entrance in bare feet and gave each of them a big hug.

Even though Mommy's health had not been getting any better and she was spending more time in bed, she managed to wake herself enough to respectfully greet and bow to her dear neighbors. Daddy and Mr. Akai were relieved to find that they were both safely home despite their injuries.

My Brother Shige

Several months passed and it was now May. Baby Shige had started to have some stomach problems. No matter how quickly we changed and washed his diapers, it was not enough. He even refused to sip on thin rice gruel. One-year old Shige had been losing more and more weight.

One late night, I heard Mommy crying while talking to Daddy in the next room.

"We have been feeding him so much koryan and he's not getting the nutrition he needs… poor baby. Only if we could feed him white rice congee…"

A few days later, Shige let out his last breath like a candle flame softly blown out at night.

The next day, on top of a wood crate in the corner of the living room, Baby Shige's urn[25] was placed next to his baby sister's smaller urn.

There lay the ashes of two flames that had been extinguished much too early from this world.

---

25   Urn: It's a small container with a lid used to store the ashes of a cremated person.

1946 September 2:

Tonghua

Leaving Tonghua

In September, over one year after the war ended, there was finally good news that my family and our neighbors could go back to our homeland.

My parents invited Mr. and Mrs. Akai over and were having what looked like an important discussion. That evening, after eating our typical koryan congee, Daddy began to speak.

"Everyone agrees that plans have been made to get us all home. Over at Huludao Port, there are ships that can take us back to Japan. It would be ideal if we could all leave together, but Mommy's health is still not well enough. I will stay behind with Mommy until she gets a little better and stronger. Hiro will be going home with Mommy and me. Misa, Mr. and Mrs. Akai have agreed to take you with them. You will be leaving in two days. Understand?"

Misa nodded.

"Daddy's colleague, Mr. Nemoto, has agreed to take Iku and Kiyoshi with him. You will be leaving with him tomorrow. There will be a train departing from Tonghua Station, so you two will be able to get a head start with the other Japanese families. This was a difficult decision to make but Mommy and I have both agreed that this is for the best. Once you make it to Huludao Port, that's easy… you only have to hop on a ship. Do whatever you can to make it home safe. We'll all be reunited back in Shizuoka soon. Do you understand?"

Tomorrow? So soon? Separately?…

My mind was filled with questions, confusion, and anxiety, but there was no choice but to listen to Daddy. Departure set for tomorrow.

Now that I thought about it, I realized that Mommy had been sitting up more hours lately, busily sewing. Even though her condition had been worsening ever since Shige's death, she was hard at work sewing new clothes for us children. She was making them from her old, leftover kimonos the Chinese soldiers hadn't taken.

"Mommy, are you ok? Are you tired?" I asked. Mommy would look at me and always smile while she continued to sew.

"There, done! You can wear this tomorrow when you leave."

Mommy's old striped kimono had been transformed into a cute little dress for me.

"I sewed in a large nametag, you see? This way you will never get lost." said Mommy. Sewed on to the chest was a large nametag that included my name and Japanese address. She had done the same on Kiyoshi's shirt.

"Iku, can you carry this backpack again?" asked Mommy. The backpack that I carried when I left Japan three and a half years ago had been hidden in the attic the whole time. The backpack still proved to be very large for my small frame, but it was now only half full. It contained a change of clothes for Kiyoshi and me, some rice crackers and roasted soy beans.

That evening, Mommy called us both to her.

"Do you want to sleep with me tonight in my futon bed? Come on, hop in!"

Kiyoshi and I nodded our heads and snuggled into Mommy's futon.

So warm…

Mommy's scent…

Kiyoshi and I laid on each side of Mommy and the three of us fell asleep holding each other's hands.

A Promise to Live For

Everyone got up early the next morning to get ready. I changed into my new white and orange striped dress that Mommy made for me. Then, Mommy handed me a small purse that I could hang around my neck.

"Here's some money for you to take. Use it only when necessary. Treat it like a good luck charm. Always keep it around your neck, ok?" said Mommy.

"Yes, Mommy."

"Also, make sure to stay with Mr. Nemoto the whole time."

"Yes, Mommy."

"Iku, never ever let go of Kiyoshi's hand. Kiyoshi, never ever let go of Iku's hand, no matter how tired you get. Understand? I need you two to promise me."

"I promise, Mommy. I won't ever let go of Kiyoshi's hand," I replied as Kiyoshi also nodded next to me. Mommy gave both of us a big, big hug. I clutched on to Mommy's frail neck and whispered, "Mommy, get well soon. I'll be waiting for you in Shizuoka."

I could feel Mommy nodding as our cheeks brushed together. I also felt Mommy's chest trembling against mine. Mommy gently held my face and then Kiyoshi's, and said, "You be careful," as tears formed in her eyes.

Kiyoshi and I stood outside the front door after we put our shoes on and waved to Mommy on her futon bed and to Misa and Hiro who were sitting by her side.

"We'll see you in Shizuoka!"

Daddy walked us to Tonghua Station. The station was packed with Japanese families who were all going back. At the entrance, we met with Mr. Nemoto. As Daddy handed over Kiyoshi and me to Mr. Nemoto, he deeply bowed his head to Mr. Nemoto and said, "I cannot thank you enough for your kind offer. Please stay safe."

As Daddy watched us disappear into the busy crowd, he prayed over and over in a thin voice.

"Please… please make it safely back to Japan."

Mommy's Tears

When Daddy returned from the station, he found Hiro innocently calling his mother while she lay still in her futon bed.

"Mommy, wake up! Mommy!"

But she was not waking up.

Misa looked up at Daddy with her face full of tears. Daddy rushed to Mommy's side and shook her shoulder but there was nothing.

She had already drawn her last breath.

Mommy was lying quietly-- so thin and fragile. The trickle of tears that had run down from her eyes was still wet to the touch.

She was thirty-three years old.

Misa spent the day over at the Akai's. Mrs. Akai took Misa's hand and gently pulled her outside to point toward the smoke that was coming from her house.

"Take a good look at the smoke, Misa," she said

softy. "Your Daddy is cremating your Mommy's body, and that's her spirit rising up in the smoke."

Hiro, sitting next to Daddy and Misa over at the Akai's house, all said their goodbyes to Mommy as they watched the white smoke drift off into the orange sunset.

It was such a sorrowful smoke and the graying sky seemed so sad to be receiving it.

1946 September 3 - September 30:

Tonghua ~ Huludao Port

The Packed Train

When we boarded the train, we found it already jam-packed and there was no roof. It was September but the sun was still hot and beat down on us without mercy. Everyone in the swaying train was filthy and sweaty.

I made sure to hold on to Kiyoshi's damp hand and sat very close to Mr. Nemoto on the floor.

From time to time the train would make stops without warning. No one had any idea whether the stop would be long or short, so many people rushed off to quickly go to the bathroom. Since there were no bathrooms on the train, everyone was forced to go right next to the train tracks or in the nearby cornfields. Many children were not able to hold it long enough in between stops, so they were forced to use anything, like small pots and bowls, that their parents carried in the train.

Not long after departing from Tonghua Station, I noticed that Mr. Nemoto looked uncomfortable. His face was distorted as he groaned in pain. He was also sweating profusely.

SCREECH!

When the train came to the next stop, Mr. Nemoto placed his hands on Kiyoshi's and my heads and looked at us silently. Without saying a word, he stood up and walked towards the exit. I watched him walk away and my eyes stopped at the top of his trousers. They were stained red with blood.

Mr. Nemoto never came back.

On the first day after leaving Tonghua, Kiyoshi and I who were just six and ten years old were suddenly left all by ourselves. I looked around the whole train car but could not recognize anyone.

How can we do this all alone?"

With my mind filled with anxiety and concern, I continued to stay close to my brother. I laid my head onto my knees and felt the train sway beneath me.

A Long Procession of Japanese

Suddenly the train came to another stop, but this time it did not continue on. We were still a long way from our final destination. Although I did not know why, all of us had to grab our belongings and step off the train.

Why? It hasn't even been a whole day since we started…

As Kiyoshi and I got off the train with the others, our only option seemed to be to follow the crowd as we walked along the train tracks in a long line. I held on tightly to Kiyoshi's hand.

"We have to walk for a while. Can you do it?"

Kiyoshi looked up at me and nodded his head. We followed the train tracks, at times crossing dirt roads and through farms.

Suddenly Kiyoshi said quietly.

"I'm hungry…"

I realized that we had not eaten anything since leaving Tonghua. We stopped for a moment so that I could take off my backpack and pulled out the rice crackers that Mommy had prepared for us; one for Kiyoshi and one for myself.

"You can't eat it all at once. Bit by bit. Ok?"

I then gave Kiyoshi a sip of water and then drank some myself. Kiyoshi followed my instructions and nibbled at the rice cracker while we continued to walk.

As we walked along the dirt road, it started to get dark. I could hear people ahead deciding to stop and rest there for the night so I decided we should stop there, too. That night, the weeds were our beds. When we looked up, the night sky was alive with bright, shiny stars.

Kiyoshi and I held our backpack between us and slept holding tightly to each other. Even though it was our first time sleeping outside, we fell soundly asleep after our long day.

As the sun began to rise, Kiyoshi and I woke up to the sound of the surrounding people getting ready for another long day ahead. I was so relieved to find my backpack safe and sound.

Kiyoshi was in a grumpy mood as soon as he

woke up and started crying. I realized why right away. He had peed his pants. Six-year old Kiyoshi still had accidents sometimes when he was asleep. I tried to comfort him and told him gently there was nothing to worry about, because there was no bed to clean.

"No worries, Kiyoshi. It's ok. Let's change."

I pulled out some clothes from the backpack and helped him change.

The Horse Carriage with a Roof

Since we could not afford to get left behind, I hurriedly put on my backpack and took Kiyoshi's hand. We started walking at the end of the group.

The second day was again filled with lots of walking in the long procession of Japanese. After a while, Kiyoshi sat down on the ground.

"I can't walk anymore…"

Without many options, I decided to sit down

next to my brother and take a break. Every now and then, a carriage would go by. While Kiyoshi and I were taking a break, the others in our group had moved on, so we had to wait for the next group. As soon as they arrived, I took my whining brother's hand, and pulled him along. However, not long after, Kiyoshi would sit down again. No matter how much I pleaded or pulled, he would refuse to stand back up. The group was getting farther and farther away. And so it went. We would have to wait for the next group, walk a little, and sit back down. Progress was painfully slow.

When the sun began rising over the horizon, we would walk as much as we could until the sun would begin to set in the west. That was our routine for days and days. Even in extreme rain, we held hands while getting soaked and kept walking. We had no other choice.

* * *

It was another hot, sunny day. We were walking, still holding hands just as we were told.

"I can't walk anymore..." said Kiyoshi as he started crying again and sat down.

"We have to keep on walking!" I replied, but Kiyoshi refused to listen.

"I want Mommy..."

"We'll get to see Mommy when we're back in Japan but we have to get there first! Please, we have to keep going!" I pleaded. I had finally convinced Kiyoshi to start walking again when we heard a carriage behind us.

I wish I could ride on a carriage. That would be so comfortable.

As the carriage passed by, I glanced over at it and my heart almost stopped.

Wait! Was that Misa?

The little girl was nonchalantly waving her hands at the groups of people she passed.

It was definitely Misa!

The carriage with a roof passed in front of me as if it was in slow motion and continued to get farther and farther away. At that moment I felt so hopeless that my legs gave way and I collapsed on the ground. As I looked up at Kiyoshi, I envied his little legs that could just keep going. I didn't want to cry, for his sake, but big tears started rolling down my face.

As I saw Little Kiyoshi innocently looking back at me, I found a reason to stand up again.

I have to be strong and keep fighting!!

I quickly wiped away my tears with the back of my hands, and grabbed Kiyoshi's hand.

"Come on! Let's go!"

Horse-drawn Carriages

Kiyoshi and I had not eaten anything substantial that day but we continued to walk. Just as we were taking a break underneath a tree, a carriage stopped and several people got off.

"Shang ma? (Want a ride?)" asked the Chinese driver.

I looked at Kiyoshi. The never ending days of walking had left our feet sore and exhausted. I decided we should hop onto the horse carriage. From the cloth purse around my neck that Mommy had given me, I pulled out a coin and gave it to the driver. He looked at it and didn't look very happy, but accepted it anyway.

"Hao hao. Shang ba! (Fine, fine. Get on!)" said the driver. Kiyoshi and I stepped towards the carriage.

An old Japanese man grabbed our arms and pulled us inside.

The carriage started. The road was far from smooth so the passengers were bouncing all over the place. Soon after, it was our turn to pass the group of people that left us behind while we were resting underneath the tree.

"Iku, carriages are so fast! This is great!"

Kiyoshi was beaming.

However, it was not too much longer when the driver stopped and turned around to collect more money.

We'll run out of money if we keep on paying…

I hopped off of the carriage.

"Kiyoshi, we have to get off."

I pulled on my brother's hand but Kiyoshi did not want to leave.

"I don't want to get off! I wanna keep riding this carriage!"

Kiyoshi started crying. I wanted to cry, too, but I held back my tears. I pulled on my stubborn brother's arm even more and forced him to step down from the carriage. I took my brother's hand firmly and started walking while Kiyoshi continued to cry.

There were many people sitting along the roadside. They could no longer walk.

We saw one mother sobbing as she dug a hole to bury a baby that had passed away. Afterwards the mother sat and quietly prayed.

As the number of days spent walking increased relentlessly, so did the number of dead bodies on the side of the road. Bodies that had been stripped of their clothes were not an uncommon sight. Many bodies didn't have shoes, either.

If I die, they're going to take away my clothes, too. I don't want to die all by myself here and get kicked around on the side of the road. I won't die. I can't die. I have to keep walking. I have to bring Kiyoshi home. Once we're in Japan, I get to see Daddy and Mommy again.

I became determined to take one step at a time, with Kiyoshi by my side, until we finally had crossed this vast landscape.

A Lost Child

We reached a long, wide bridge that spanned a large river. As soon as he saw the bridge, Kiyoshi refused to walk any farther and sat down crying. No matter how much I pleaded with him, he would not listen. I was so exhausted that there was no way I would be able to carry him. I looked around and spotted a carriage in the distance. I looked in the purse.

There's still some money left…

I decided to send Kiyoshi on the carriage. Once I told him that he could ride on it, he finally stopped crying.

"You wait for me as soon as you finish crossing the bridge, ok? Don't go anywhere from there. Got it?"

Kiyoshi stepped up onto the carriage and left. I tried as best as I could to run and keep up, but the horse's speed proved to be way too fast. The carriage disappeared into the crowd as it got farther and farther away.

I pushed myself to reach the end of the bridge quickly so I could meet up with Kiyoshi. However, Kiyoshi was nowhere to be seen.

Had he been taken by someone?

"Kiyoshi! Kiyoshi!"

I yelled at the top of my lungs.

"Kiyoshi!! Kiyoshi!!"

I was becoming frantic.

What have I done? Oh no… If I never find Kiyoshi, Mommy and Daddy will be really mad at me. I would never be able to face them. I failed to keep my promise to Mommy. Why did I let him go? Oh no…

"Excuse me… have you seen a little boy? He's six years old. He was on a carriage and was supposed to get off here… did you see him get off?"

I asked several people that passed by but was only met with shaking heads.

What to do, what to do…

I couldn't decide whether to go back on the bridge, or wait here, or look ahead.

Maybe he wasn't able to get off of the carriage and had to continue on it!

I decided to keep going to look for my brother.

Suddenly, I overheard a lady next to me say, "Poor boy… he was all by himself. I wonder if he's lost… or his family is all gone…"

What was that? A boy?

"Excuse me… how old was the boy?" I asked.

"He looked like he was still too young to attend

school. He had a big nametag on his chest. He was crying in the middle of the bridge," replied the lady.

Maybe… it might be Kiyoshi! A big nametag! It had to be Kiyoshi!

I bowed to the lady and turned around. I headed for the bridge, against the flow of traffic, my large backpack bouncing right and left on my back.

"Kiyoshi! Kiyoshi!"

I yelled as I ran.

"Kiyoshi!! Kiyoshi!!"

"Iku! Iku!"

I heard the cries of a little boy.

Kiyoshi…! Where are you?

I ran towards the direction where the voice was coming from.

It's him! Kiyoshi!

I spotted my little brother along the bridge-rail.

"Kiyoshi!!"

When Kiyoshi saw me in the crowd, he started to cry very loudly.

"Iku… Iku…"

I dashed to my little brother. I held him as tightly as I could so that I wouldn't lose him ever again. A huge relief rushed over me as tears rolled down my cheeks.

After calming down, Kiyoshi took a big breath and said,

"I'm hungry. Can I have a rice cracker?"

I pulled out one rice cracker and placed it on his small palm. Kiyoshi took small bites out of his rice cracker and started to speak softly.

"When I couldn't see you, I got scared… so I got off…"

I replied as if I was talking to myself.

"No matter what happens, I'm not letting go of your hand. We're going to keep our promise to Mommy and make it home to Shizuoka! Until we get to see her, I'm not letting go of your hand! Never!!"

Never!!!

I was determined to keep true to my word.

After a short rest, we got back up on our feet. I grasped Kiyoshi's little hand tightly. Kiyoshi squeezed back just as hard.

Since that incident, Kiyoshi never again complained that he couldn't walk anymore, no matter how tired he was. We used all our strength and kept walking.

Walk, stop for rest, then walk again.

We pushed ourselves to keep up with each new group. When evening came, we sandwiched my backpack between us and fell asleep under the vast starlit sky.

The Port and the Ocean

It was just another day of walking under the baking sun when I overheard a man talking to his family in front of us.

"If we can walk just a little bit longer, it sounds like there's a station where we can catch a train. I know your feet hurt but keep going for just a little bit longer... just a little bit more."

Kiyoshi had been listening in, too, and he quickly looked up at me.

A train station!

We suddenly began to get new energy and no longer dragged our feet. I firmly took my brother's hand, gritted my teeth, and pushed ourselves to keep up with the others.

Eventually, we did see a train station in the distance. A roofless train was stopped, but it was already quite full. Kiyoshi and I were forced to walk to the very end of the train to step up onto the open deck of a flatcar. There were no walls or supports to prevent people from falling off, so all the adults formed a wall around the children.

"We're almost there. Just a little bit and we'll arrive at Huludao and get on the ship headed for Japan. We can do it," said the man I heard earlier. Those positive words resonated in my heart.

How long were we on the train? It would stop, then run a little bit, and stop again. I was so exhausted that I got confused how many hours, or even days, that we were on the train.

I felt the train suddenly shake so I opened my eyes. Everyone started moving around to gather their belongings and got ready to get off. The thought of still more walking made my legs feel so heavy. The man who had encouraged us earlier spoke again, almost as if he could read my mind.

"We've arrived at the port of Huludao[26]. Look! That may be our ship. Or maybe that one. You two can follow me."

The port was teeming with people, so it didn't look like we would be able to board a ship right away. First everyone had to go through a medical examination and be vaccinated several times.

While we waited in the long line, I looked at my feet and then at Kiyoshi's. The little bit of material that was left barely resembled shoes anymore and our filthy

---

26   Huludao: It was the main port city that was used to transfer the Japanese refugees from China to Japan. When WWII ended, it is said there were about 1.5 million Japanese people left in China, mostly in the northeastern part. On May 7, 1946, the first ship left the port for Japan carrying 2489 Japanese people. From then until August, 1948, an average of seven ships left for Japan every day carrying some 2000 people per ship. In all, around 1,050,000 Japanese went through this port to go back to their homeland.

feet that stuck out the front had overgrown, broken toenails.

We finally reached the baggage check, but all that was left in my backpack were our dirty clothes. The kind man from the train saw our confusion, looked at our nametags and quickly filled out all the paperwork. He also directed us to the right place to board the ship. It was finally time to get ready to get on to the ship.

Just before we walked up the plank, I took a moment to look behind me. One month[27] had passed since we left Tonghua.

We had walked 550 kilometers (340 miles), essentially traveling the distance between Tokyo Station and Shin-Osaka Station (between Boston and Philadelphia, or between San Francisco and Los Angeles) to reach the coast.

We'll get to see Mommy soon...

I turned and looked forward again. I saw the ocean--the big, big ocean.

The other side of the ocean lay Japan...

Grandpa with his pipe tobacco sitting in his usual spot...

---

27   one month: What were Iku and Kiyoshi eating during the month they were walking across Manchuria? The small amount of food that their mother packed in their backpack was obviously not enough to keep them alive for a whole month. It is possible that they ate some grass along the road. They might have eaten some vegetables growing in the fields along the way. A few adults might have shared some of their food with Iku and Kiyoshi. However, neither of them can remember any other food that they ate besides the rice crackers and roasted soybeans that their mother had prepared.

Grandma who often gave me dried bananas…

Aunt Yuki in front of her sewing machine…

Uncle So who taught me the Japanese alphabet and how to tell time…

Masaki who always walked to kindergarten with me…

And finally, Mommy, Daddy, Misa, and Hiro…

We'll soon be reunited with everyone again…

We are on our way, everyone…!

1946 September 30 - October 9:

On the Ship

Meiyu-maru

Meiyu-maru was docked directly in front of where Kiyoshi and I were standing. For all of us, that ship meant hope… and home. Kiyoshi and I followed the crowd that was moving, one by one, up the gangway. The more than three thousand people that boarded the Meiyu-maru that day were leaving the old life in Manchuria behind and walking into a new life in Japan as they took those first steps on the gangway.

The inside of the ship had been altered to accommodate the large number of people. An extra floor had been created that resembled one huge bunk bed. As huge as the ship was, it was still jam-packed inside. Everyone fought to claim their own space to sit and sleep. Kiyoshi and I were told to go to the upper floor. We had to fend for ourselves to find a space, and it needed to be large enough for us to straighten our legs.

A Sake Bottle

Even though the people who boarded the ship were one step closer to home, the days on the ship were in no way pleasant. The food rations consisted of dried bread and a few grains of rice that barely made a thin porridge.

On the second day, early in the morning, the old man underneath Kiyoshi and me started shouting angrily and woke us up. Kiyoshi had accidentally peed his pants again in his sleep and it had seeped through the thin wooden boards and was dripping onto the lower bunk.

"We have to do something. I'm going to run up to the upper deck so you stay here and guard our spot, ok?" I told my little brother and started walking around the ship by myself to find a solution for the problem.

How do I fix this problem? What should I do?

As I walked around the upper deck, I noticed several people quietly crowding around something and sobbing. I wondered what was happening so I walked towards the crowd. I saw something wrapped in an old gunny sack placed on a board. A few seconds later the board was tilted and the sack slid into the ocean. Then a voice cried out.

"Mommy! Mommy!"

The mournful sound of the fog horn spread across the ocean and the ship made a couple of big circles as if saying goodbye.

That image of an old gunny sack sliding down into the ocean floated back into my thoughts as a shiver went through my body.

I don't want to die... I don't want to be left alone in the cold, dark ocean... No matter what, Kiyoshi and I have to reach Japan alive!

I quickly got back on task and started exploring the inside of the ship. As the ship swayed to one side, I heard a little sound.

clink…

It was an empty sake[28] bottle.

"That's it!" I exclaimed. "It's this! This is it!"

I grabbed the empty bottle and ran back to Kiyoshi. He looked confused when he saw the empty bottle.

That bottle ended up preventing any future incidents until we got off the ship. Every night, I would wake up my sleeping brother to make sure he went to the bathroom in the bottle. The old man underneath never got mad at us again.

---

28   sake: It's a Japanese rice wine.

Kiyoshi Giving Back

The ship approached the Genkai Sea[29] where the relentless waves caused the ship to constantly sway left and right. I was prone to seasickness and felt sick in my stomach. A woman sitting nearby saw my pale face and said, "It might be a good idea to go up to the upper deck to get some fresh air. I'll tell you what. I can keep an eye on your spot, so go ahead and help your sister, young boy."

We nodded our heads in thanks, and climbed up the steep stairs to the upper deck. Kiyoshi kept a worried eye on me and sat very close. Whenever there was a huge wave, the ship would rock and splash seawater on our faces. I couldn't bear any more and threw up all over my clothes. There was nothing to do but take off my dress. Suddenly, Kiyoshi grabbed my dress and walked off with it. Being confused, I turned my head to see where he was going, only to find him walking towards the small water station in the corner of the deck. He sat down next to a bucket of clean

---

29   Genkai Sea: It's a sea located off the northwestern coast of Japan's Kyushu island.

seawater and quickly got to work.

splash… splat… splash… splat…

I could hear the splashes of my six-year old brother hard at work, swaying right and left as the ship swayed. His small hands were scrubbing my tattered dress.

We had endured four long days when we heard shouts coming from the deck.

"Land, ho! I can see land!"

"It's land! It's land!"

"Hurrah!"

Everyone on the ship, who had suffered a long journey alike, celebrated with joy and shared relief like one big, happy family. The woman that was kind to Kiyoshi and me patted us on the head and praised us.

"You two have done an extraordinary job to get here all by yourselves. Great job!"

1946 October 9:

Sasebo Port

Japan for the First Time in Three Years

The day[30] we had all been waiting for had finally come.

"It's time!"

"We've come home! Our home!"

The crowd was filled with excitement and smiles could be seen everywhere as people stepped down onto the gangway. I took Kiyoshi's hand and followed everyone off the ship. On that day, September 9th, 1946, 3014 refugees[31] from Manchuria

---

30   the day: After arriving at the port, the ships were not allowed to let the people off for several days. They were quarantined long enough to be sure no one was carrying a disease that might spread through the country.

31   3014 refugees: This number was obtained by contacting the Uragashira Repatriate Memorial Museum.

disembarked the Meiyu-maru and set foot on Japanese soil.

As soon as we stepped off the gangway, we were met with a huge chemical spray. I gasped. In order to exterminate any parasites and ticks, everyone was sprayed with a chemical called DDT. We were covered from head to toe with the fine, white powder, even under our shirt collars and inside sleeves.

After the pest extermination came customs. The nametags that Mommy had sewed on our clothes proved to be extremely useful again.

"Ando-cho, Shizuoka City, Shizuoka. Ok, I'll send a telegram to this address. It'll be a good idea to stay at the Repatriation Support Bureau where you can clean up and rest. I'll let you know when the train for Shizuoka will leave. You must be exhausted… you deserve some good rest," said a man as he kindly helped us.

"You, too, little guy. Coming back all this way to Japan with your big sister... good job… indeed, good job."

Kiyoshi grinned from ear to ear as the man praised him and patted his head.

With customs taken care of, Kiyoshi and I headed to the Repatriation Support Bureau. I paused for a moment on the way to take some big, deep breaths.

There are no more Chinese or Russian soldiers to be scared of...

No more gun shots…

This is my homeland!

"Kiyoshi, we get to sleep with our legs stretched out as much as we want tonight!" I said excitedly. Just that one little luxury made me so happy.

"Kiyoshi, we'll get to see Mommy again! Soon… yes, very soon..."

1946 Octoer 13:

Shizuoka

Haenosaki Station

Three days after arriving at Sasebo Port, we left the Repatriation Support Bureau and headed to Haenosaki Station. We were divided into groups according to province and got tickets for our respective destinations before we boarded the trains.

The train Kiyoshi and I had boarded gave a sharp whistle and departed. Inside the train, there were many kinds of people who were headed in the same direction as us, and they helped us transfer to Shizuoka.

Passengers came and went as we stopped at various stations. We saw the ocean, went through tunnels, and sat through the hours-long train ride.

Night fell, and morning came again. A woman next to us tapped us on the shoulder and said, "Next is Shizuoka. You should get ready to get off soon."

The mountains started to look familiar. Shizuhata Mountain, where the Sengen Shrine is, could be easily recognized.

My home, Shizuoka!

I've dreamed of you for so long!

Our Home, Shizuoka

"Hey! Iku! Iku and Kiyoshi!"

Uncle So, pulling a cart, was waving his hand and calling our names.

"Uncle So!"

"You're here! You're safe!"

He knelt down and kept patting our heads. We could see that his eyes were full of tears.

Relief flooded over me and I fell asleep in Uncle So's swaying cart during the thirty-minute trip home. I started dreaming. We are in Manchuria. At our home in Manchuria, the whole family is gathered for dinner. The dinner table is filled with dishes. Our bowls are filled with rice, not porridge. Baby Shige is eating all by himself. Mommy is helping Hiro get more miso soup that he loves so much. Daddy is carefully taking the small bones out of the fish.

"Iku, Iku. We're here," said Uncle So, waking me from my dream.

"Iku and Kiyoshi are here!"

Grandpa and Grandma came rushing out the door.

"You are home! You're safely home!" they exclaimed. "The journey must have been so difficult. The two of you, what you've done is so amazing! We are so proud of you."

There were no words that could describe the

deep emotions we felt, so we just looked at one another silently.

The Three Urns

Grandma took my hand and I stepped into Grandpa's house for the first time in three years.

It smelled like Grandpa's house.

I could smell the rice that Grandma was cooking.

The aroma of roasting sweet potatoes filled the room.

We really did make it home…

I was still at the doorstep and found myself unable to move. Suddenly, I heard footsteps running down the hall and Misa popped around the corner.

"Misa!" I exclaimed.

"Hurry up, Iku! Come with me! Daddy's waiting!"

Daddy? He's already here? With Mommy and Hiro? What? Everyone already made it home?

I quickly took off my shoes and followed Misa. I found Daddy in the next room with the sliding doors all the way open. I looked at him sitting on the futon bed. He had lost weight and his cheeks were sunken. Hiro sat next to him, and his head seemed too large for his little body. He had been malnourished for so long that he was not able to stand, and was weakly leaning against Daddy.

"We are home!"

And then, Kiyoshi and I looked for Mommy.

"Where's Mommy? Mommy got better so she doesn't need to be in bed anymore? Is that right? Where is she?" I asked Daddy.

He only replied with a small shake of his head. A look of sorrow crossed his eyes. Instead of Daddy, it was Misa who spoke up.

"Mommy died…"

"What?"

Daddy silently pointed towards the altar where three urns were placed.

"Why? Why three? Is Mommy's one of them? No! It can't be Mommy's! She promised that we'd reunite in Shizuoka!" I cried.

Daddy pulled Kiyoshi and me down beside him and began to tell us all that had happened after he got back from Tonghua Station that day. Kiyoshi and I knelt down and hung on every word.

After Daddy finished, he asked, "Why didn't Mr. Nemoto bring you here? Did he have to head for home after he handed you two over to Uncle So at the station?"

I shook my head.

"After leaving Tonghua Station, Mr. Nemoto disappeared… we waited for him but he never came back… it was just Kiyoshi and me the whole time…"

"What?"

There was a long silence.

"Iku…"

Then Daddy broke down and cried, pulling us both close to him, ever so tightly.

"Iku, Kiyoshi, why don't you two offer some incense to the altar to let your Mommy, Shige and your baby sister know you're home and you're safe," said Grandpa. I sat down in front of Mommy's picture that was placed at the altar. My eyes met with Mommy's. She seemed to be looking straight at me with her soft, gentle smile. Next to the picture were the beanbags that Mommy had made.

Mommy… I'm home. I held Kiyoshi's hand and… I kept your promise… we walked and walked and walked all the way here so I could see you again… Mommy… Mommy…

"Mommy!!"

My heart filled with grief. I just kept calling for Mommy over and over and over.

The White Shiny Onigiri

"It's so white!" Kiyoshi exclaimed. I turned around as I wiped away my tears and noticed three big, round onigiri that Grandma had made and placed on the table. The steam was still rising off them. They were so white that they were almost blinding me, and I saw each and every grain of rice sparkling brightly.

It was the first time in years that I had seen white onigiri.

Kiyoshi and I each took one. Kiyoshi couldn't wait and took a big bite, forgetting to say grace. I looked at the gleaming onigiri. It seemed at first too precious to eat, but then I was overcome by the wonderful aroma that wafted upwards with the steam. Saying grace quickly, I took a bite. And another bite. The subtle sweet taste of the white rice filled my mouth. It was such a perfectly round and fluffy onigiri.

Still, we finished those onigiri in record time. I grabbed the last one left on the plate and split it in half and, as usual, gave the larger piece to my little brother. This time, we made sure to take our time chewing and enjoying it, grain by grain. As we finished eating, our tummies began to feel as warm as our hearts.

After watching us eat our food so happily, Daddy stood up and left the room. As he passed the kitchen, he heard Grandma softly sobbing. He looked closer and saw her clutching something from my backpack.

It was my white and orange striped dress that Mommy had made from one of her old kimonos. The hem was tattered and the colors were so faded that it was hard to tell where the stripes were.

Without words, the dress revealed the pain and suffering that we had endured on the journey home.

That evening, I took a long bath for the first time in several years. In the dressing room, I removed the purse that was hanging from my neck that Mommy had hung when we left Tonghua. I pulled it off slowly, as if it were a good luck charm that needed to be handled carefully. Even though the purse string, made from an old kimono scrap, was so faded that the patterns were indistinguishable, this purse had endured everything with me, and I felt extremely attached to it. It was a memento of Mommy. I carefully placed it on my folded clothes and stepped into the bathroom[32].

I scrubbed and cleaned my hair, washing away years of dirt and grime. It was as if all the suffering and exhaustion I endured since the war ended washed away along with the dirt and grime. I slid into the warm bathtub and realized that this was the first time in over a year that I felt so relaxed and surrounded by warmth. When I was in preschool, I would sing loudly in the bathtub and the room echoed with my energy. But this night, I listened to the sound of the steam droplets falling from the ceiling into the water and to the little crackles and pops coming from the firewood while I quietly tucked in my knees in the tub. I felt like I could melt away into the warm water. The sudden

---

32   bathroom: A typical Japanese bathroom has a wash space and a deep tub. You must wash your body first before getting into a deep tub to relax. That way, the water stays clean and can be reused by other family members.

rush of relief and joy overwhelmed me. When I felt tears begin to fall, I quickly rinsed my face as if someone would notice and I would feel embarrassed.

After drying off, I changed into fresh nightwear that Grandma had prepared for me. It was the first time in a long time that clothes felt so clean. Kiyoshi, who had taken a bath earlier with Grandpa, had been given a haircut. With his new buzz cut, Kiyoshi was completely transformed. In the bedroom, on each side of Daddy's futon was one for each of us. During our long month of lying on the fields and sleeping on the hard surfaces in the ship, Kiyoshi and I had dreamed of laying on a soft, fluffy futon again. Here it was now in front of us and the dream had finally come true.

Across the warm futon that smelled of the warm sun, I glanced at Mommy's smiling picture on the altar.

Mommy, we made it home. It was so hard but I now know that you were watching over us the whole time. Thank you. I want to see you, Mommy… I want to fall asleep holding your warm hand… I want to put

my cheek against your cheek that always smelled so
comforting… Mommy… I miss you…

Tears gave way to sleep--a peaceful sleep.

October 13th, 1946, the day Kiyoshi and I safely
arrived to Shizuoka, was more than a year after the end
of the war. It was not until that day that the war had
truly ended for my brother Kiyoshi and me.

2016 New Year Holidays:

Shizuoka

Epilogue

"And, this is the story of when I was called Iku," said Grandma. The grandchildren who had been listening so intently were left without words.

"You know… I don't want anyone to have to suffer and endure anything like this ever again. I want the world to be a place where everyone can live in peace and joy. That is my great wish," Grandma said. She stood up and pulled something out of a chest drawer.

"This is Mommy," she said while holding up a black and white picture in an old frame.

"Iku's Mommy…" Kai said softly while looking

at the picture. In Kai's little hand, Grandma placed two beanbags that had long lost their colors. He gently turned over the beanbags on his palm. The sound of the dried red beans softly filled his ears.

"It's been seventy years since I pushed myself so hard to finish the journey and to see my family. And look now! I'm surrounded by my wonderful grandchildren and I couldn't be happier. I have no doubt that Mommy is still looking over us to this day," Grandma said. She stroked the familiar fabric of the beanbags on Kai's hand and slowly closed her eyes.

Deep in her thoughts, Mommy appeared. She stood there, with her gentle smile, holding Shige and her baby girl in a field of dandelions.

Words from Iku

It's been almost 72 years since I came back from Manchuria. That 10-year old little girl turned 82 this year.

I feel very blessed because most days are peaceful and calm. Clear blue sky, green trees, chirping sounds of birds, colorful flowers in the yard… they have been around me for all these years but I feel that it's only recently that I truly felt the beauty of nature from the bottom of my heart.

Feeling this beautiful nature in front of me, as I close my eyes, the scenes from the time when my family was in Manchuria keep pouring from my mind… corn and koryan fields, bluish white fire balls rising into the air from the valley, dead bodies left on the street, looking at the shining stars as I tried to fall asleep in the field, rough seas and splashing waves against the deck…

How did a 10-year old girl and her 6-year old brother manage to come back to Shizuoka, Japan by themselves? There must have been so many kind people who helped us along the way. Please allow me to take this opportunity to say "thank you" to those people who protected and gave a hand to us.

As we prepared to publish this book, I was forced to confront my past after a long time. This was not easy for me as many painful and sad memories that were buried in a very deep part of my heart were brought to the surface.

"What if there had not been a war?" I cursed my derailed life. "What if my mother didn't die?" I suddenly felt this sorrow again, causing tears to roll down my cheeks. However, with this book being published, I think everything will be washed away and purified, and it will help me finally end the war within myself.

In this book, I recollected stories and events in which Chinese and Soviet soldiers killed Japanese people, but I just want to make it clear that I do not hold any ill feelings toward anyone. I fully realize Japanese soldiers committed atrocities against Chinese and other people as well. My point in the book is that war is our common enemy and leads to so much suffering, hatred, and hardship.

WAR. How can only a three-letter word bring such massive ache and scars in people's hearts? Looking back on my childhood, I can't help but cry as my heart aches and my feelings are crushed with pain. "WAR" can only bring "suffering" and "hatred" but can never bring "happiness" to people's minds. War takes many precious lives. The scars in our hearts keep living with us even after the war. We can never forget the reason why we are living happily today. It is because of the sacrifices that so many other people made in past wars. Nature has given human beings cognitive skills and communication tools. We need to utilize these special gifts. Each generation needs to tell the next generation about the horrors of war and why it should not be the solution to solve differences between countries. We need to realize weapons cannot bring peace to the world.

I hope the readers of this book will act to spread world peace within their own households, schools, society, and even across the globe.

I would like to pray for those who died before they could return to their homeland and to make a promise that I will live my life fully for them.

There are many people who have helped in publishing this book including Ms. Masuda from Pencom and Ms. Kurisu. It was not possible to come this far without everyone's help. My heart is filled with appreciation and thankfulness.

Lastly to my daughter, Izumi… she had been asking me to co-publish a book based on my personal experiences for seven to eight years but I was not able to commit myself.

In June of 2014, Izumi planned a trip to visit my other childhood home, in northeast China, formerly called Manchuria. For the first time in 68 years, I walked around the area where my family used to live. I visited the temple up on the hill and offered prayers. My tears didn't stop falling for a long time. Mixed emotions filled my heart, but I was very grateful that I could visit there while I was still alive.

After coming back from that trip, Izumi started researching even more intensively by reading up on more books and papers, contacting libraries and government offices, and interviewing relatives and myself over and over, and she finally brought everything together into one book. A 10-year old girl had never imagined that such a day would come after 70 years.

Izumi, thank you so much from the bottom of my heart. I hope you will continue conveying the message of the importance of peace from one person to the next.

Please allow me to show my appreciation to my grandson, Douglas, for working on the translation. You have contributed to world peace by helping spread this book all around the world.

I dream of the day when everyone in the world looks up in the blue sky where lots and lots of colorful balloons are flying as a celebration of world peace.

With deepest prayers and bright wishes for the future,
Ikue (Iku) Mochizuki
Shizuoka, Japan
July, 2018

Words from the Author

The heroine in this book, "Iku", is my mother.

Ever since I was a little girl, my mother didn't hesitate to talk about her life in Manchuria and her experiences after Japan's loss in World War II. That's why the words "Manchuria" and "repatriation" were very familiar to me even though I was born more than 20 years after the war ended.

As Japan and China resumed diplomatic relations in 1972, these two countries worked together to reunite those Japanese who were left behind in China and had lived as Chinese with their families in Japan. It was broadcasted on TV and those men and women in simple Mao suits were describing how they were left behind and recalling anything they could remember about their childhood with their Japanese families. My mother always had to turn off the TV when this program started, saying her life overlapped with theirs and she couldn't bear hearing their cries.

The story in this book finishes as two young children safely returned to their grandparents' house in Shizuoka, but even in Japan, their hardship continued as they had to start their lives from scratch, readjust to their new life, and recover from their odyssey, both physically and mentally; Iku ended up being hospitalized as a result of her harsh journey. Iku's father tried to commit suicide after feeling there was no way out. There was bullying in school and the community against those who came back from Manchuria. There were many difficult adjustments for Iku entering into a relationship with her stepmother when her father remarried. Iku's teenage period was nothing but challenging.

The main reason why I studied Chinese during my university years was because I wanted to visit my mother's childhood home. After college, I went on to get my master's degree at a university in the US, got married, and moved around to different countries due to my husband's job while raising our two boys. As the years went by, however, my dream of visiting Manchuria with my mother continued to stay with me.

In the early summer of 2014, my long-time dream finally came true while my family and I were living in Beijing, China. My father, my husband, and our younger son joined my mother and me as we headed north from Beijing. Our first stop was Tonghua where my mother's family used to live.

The city had changed dramatically since 1946 and there was little evidence of the Japanese influence anymore, but our local guide helped us locate the area where Iku's home once stood. We viewed the flow of the Hujiang River and finally visited the temple up on a hill. We purchased some long and thick Chinse-style incense and prayed as we placed it at the altar.

My mother prayed to her mother who passed away at the age of 33, and to her brother, Shige, who died of indigestion, as well as to her baby sister who died before she was even named. She remembered their faces and felt their spirits as she prayed. "I'm finally here to bring you back to Japan with me after 68 years. Let's go home now…"

Iku praying at a temple called Yuhuang Shan

View of current Tonghua-city from the top of Yuhuang Shan

After Tonghua, we visited a small town called Ji'an which is on the border between China and North Korea. The Yalu River serves as the border and there are still several bridges over it that Iku's father, my grandfather, was involved in during their construction, and those bridges are still used daily between the two countries. As my mother overlooked the river, she again prayed thinking about her father who passed away at the age of 85.

One of the bridges over the Yalu River.
The other side of the river is North Korea.

After this trip, my desire to publish a book on my mother's experiences became even stronger. This is not a story about the infamous air raids, atomic bombs or kamikaze pilots. This is not a story about Nazi concentration camps or the Pearl Harbor attack, either. However, I wanted people to know that at a place called Manchuria, there were people who suffered and died as a result of the war. I also realized how important it is to pass on these stories to the following generations so that people won't forget how horrible war is and to emphasize we should not make the same mistakes. I believe that facing and accepting the actual historical facts will lead to world peace.

When I told my mother about my intention of writing a book about her past, I asked her to draw some pictures for it. She is far from a professional, but she drew many pictures of what she remembered from her childhood. It was such a painful process for her as she dug into her past and rekindled painful memories from so long ago. My father told me there had been times when my mother was crying like a child as she drew. There were times when I regretted asking her to do such an emotionally trying task, but my mother told me that it was her duty to pass on what happened in history to the generations to come.

This book was a product of collaborative work between my mother and myself. However, I feel that there was another person who was always guiding us along through this process. I felt that my mother's mother, "Mommy" in this book, my grandmother whom I've never met, was always beside us encouraging us as we worked. With my son being involved in the translation, I think this book is a proud product of four generations.

The summer of 2017, ten months after the Japanese version was published, my mother and I visited Sasebo Port in

Nagasaki where she and her little brother returned on the Mei-yu-maru and set foot after a one-month long journey back to their homeland. Where the Repatriation Support Bureau used to be is now a big amusement park, but the Uragashira Repatriate Memorial Museum by the port kept many photos and other displays to show how the Japanese refugees from overseas, like Iku and Kiyoshi, were treated after they returned to Japanese soil. There was a big monument at the port to honor those who have safely returned and to pray for those whose lives unfortunately ended before returning to their homeland.

Iku in front of the monument at Sasebo Port, Japan

We also visited Haenosaki Station where my mother and her little brother took a train back to their hometown, Shizuoka. This station used to be a crowded hub for the refugees in the late 1940's but today it is an unstaffed station where there is hardly anyone around. While I stood at the empty platform at the station, I closed my eyes and tried to bring myself back to 1946 and to look for little Iku and Kiyoshi there. As I opened my eyes, I found my mother sitting on an old rusty bench with her eyes closed. I was certain in my heart that she was meeting her 10 years old self then.

Iku sitting on an old bench at Haenosaki Station

Mother… thank you for agreeing and making a big commitment to publish a book about your personal story. It caused you to resurface many painful and sad memories, and I know it made you cry, but I am so proud and honored that we co-produced this book which accomplished one of our life goals. It was the 70th anniversary of you and your family coming back to Japan from Manchuria when the Japanese version was published and I consider the book as a gift from me to you who were turning 80 that special year.

Here is a toast to my mother's life which she has lived fully with all her might!

Here is another toast wishing my mother many years of happiness to come!

Izumi Mochizuki Greubel

July, 2018

Special Acknowledgement

After the Japanese version of this book was published in October, 2016, many of my non-Japanese friends and relatives have asked me to work on an English one. When I told my mother this, she asked one of my sons, Douglas, to translate the Japanese book into English. He was very happy and honored to be a part of this project, especially for his grandmother whom he loves so much. Then, my husband, Tony, helped me edit Douglas' work. Thank you for being so supportive and patient during this special journey. My other son, Christopher, comforted my mother on our trip to Tonghua and he has been very supportive and encouraging throughout the whole process. My great appreciation to all of them as it is truly a family project focused on preserving the history of my mother's family.

Another shout for my appreciation goes to my dear friend, Suzi Wolfe. Suzi and her late husband, Donald "Wolfie" Wolfe, who are former colleagues of mine, were the ones who encouraged me to write this book back in 1996 when my mother first met them and told her story to them over a dinner table. Suzi was very careful with details and helped me edit the English version. Although Wolfie has since passed away, both Suzi and I know that he was looking over us while we worked on this project. We also know he is very proud that this book is finally getting published.

I want to reemphasize that this book has no intention to judge who was on the right side and who was on the wrong side during the war or who was crueler than the other. "WAR" is our enemy and the only enemy.

I would like to share a quote by Benjamin Ferencz, the last surviving prosecutor at the Nuremberg trials.

" War makes murderers out of otherwise decent people. All wars, and all decent people."

July, 2018 Izumi Mochizuki Greubel

Iku and Izumi celebrating the Japanese version
being published in Japan in October, 2016

Poem by Ikue Mochizuki

Under the bright sunshine

Appear letters of P.E.A.C.E in the blue sky

Traveling around the world carried by clouds

Children's smile, too, traveling around the world carried by balloons

One, two, three, and one more, and another one

Letters of P.E.A.C.E

Happy smiles without wars

No need of tears of sorrow, hatred, and suffering

Only wishing for smiles filled with happiness

Everyone, talk about peace!

Everyone, take each other's hand!

And let's walk on a rainbow over the world

The world filled with smiles

Peace without wars

We can't take away children's smiles

We can't let children suffer

WORLD PEACE filled with happiness

Let everyone's wish spread around the world

お日様の光に輝き
青空に描かれた平和の文字
雲にのって世界をまわる
子供達の笑顔・風船にのって世界へ
一つ・二つ・三つ・どんどんふえる
描かれた平和の文字
戦争がないからみんな幸福な笑顔
憎しみ・悲しみ・苦しみの涙はいらない
ほしいのは喜び幸福の笑顔だけ
みんなで語ろう　幸福を
みんなでつなごう　手と手を
大きな大きな虹にみんなでのろうよ
世界中　笑顔一杯
戦争のない平和
子供の笑顔と消さず
子供の涙を見ず
みんな喜び一杯の世界平和
戦争のない世界。
みんなの願い
笑顔一杯　世界に広がる
望月郁江

143

Izumi Mochizuki Greubel

Izumi was born and raised in Shizuoka-city, Japan. After graduating from university in Japan, she attended a graduate school in the United States and received a Master's degree in secondary education. She taught Japanese at the University of Southern Indiana for ten years until her husband, Tony, was hired by the U.S. Department of State. Since then, they have lived in Washington, D.C., Indonesia, Canada, Pakistan/Japan, China, and Samoa. Izumi and Tony have two sons, Douglas at Virginia Tech (class of 2018) and Christopher at the U.S. Naval Academy (class of 2021).

Ikue "Iku" Mochizuki

Ikue was born in Shizuoka-city, Japan, in 1936. She moved to Manchuria when she was six years old with her family due to her father's job as a civil engineer. She was nine years old when World War II ended in 1945. She and her little brother came back to Japan from Manchuria in 1946 by themselves after a one-month long dangerous journey. She married her husband, Takao, and they raised three children, Izumi being the first child. They also have five grandchildren; one of the five, Douglas, translated the original Japanese edition of this book into English. Ikue is living in Shizuoka-city, Japan with her husband enjoying their retirement.

footnotes

A PROMISE TO LIVE FOR

~ The story of how two small children had to trek all alone across Manchuria in 1946 ~

Izumi Mochizuki Greubel

Illustrated by Ikue "Iku" Mochizuki

English translation by Douglas Mochizuki Greubel

First edition 1st printing August 1, 2018
Author Izumi Mochizuki Greubel
Design Tsutomi Miyata
publisher Yukimi Masuda / Pencom Co., Ltd.
2-20 Hitomarucho, Akashi-shi Hyogo Prefecture 673-0877 http://pencom.co.jp
Release Impress Corporation
105, 1 - chome, Kanda Jimbocho, Chiyoda ku Tokyo 101 - 0051 Tokyo
Copyright 2018 Izumi Mochizuki Greubel
ISBN 978-4-295-40229-9 C8095

To comment, request to purchase the book, and any other inquiries,
please send an email to "apromisetolivefor@gmail.com"
or visit https://www.facebook.com/apromisetolivefor/

FOR JAPAN USE

［本の内容に関するお問い合わせ先］
株式会社ペンコム　TEL:078-914-0391　FAX:078-959-8033　office@pencom.co.jp

［乱丁本・落丁本などのお問い合わせ先］
TEL:03-6837-5016　FAX:03-6837-5023　service@impress.co.jp
（受付時間／ 10:00-12:00、13:00-17:00 土日、祝日を除く）
※古書店で購入されたものについてはお取り替えできません。

［書店／販売店様のご注文窓口］
株式会社インプレス受注センター
TEL:048-449-8040　FAX:048-449-8041
株式会社インプレス出版営業部　TEL: 03-6837-4635

印刷・製本　株式会社シナノパブリッシングプレス
©2018 Izumi Mochizuki Greubel Printed in Japan　　ISBN 978-4-295-40229-9　C8095